Introduction TO CONFLICT Management

IMPROVING PERFORMANCE USING THE TKI®

KENNETH W. THOMAS

The **Myers-Briggs**
Company

The Myers-Briggs Company
+1 800 624 1765 | www.themyersbriggs.com

Printed in the United States of America.
22 21 20   33 32 31 30 29

CONTENTS

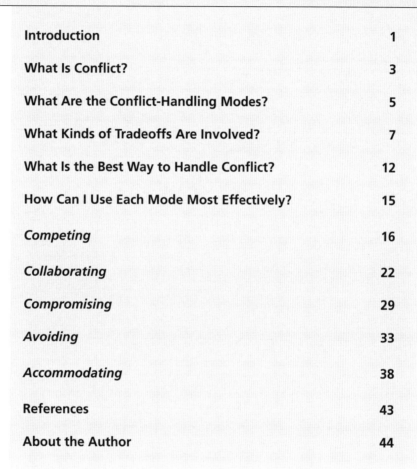

INTRODUCTION

If you recently took the *Thomas-Kilmann Conflict Mode Instrument* (TKI®), this booklet is for you. It is a next step in understanding your TKI scores and improving your ability to handle conflict effectively.

First, the booklet will help you gain a better grasp of the five conflict-handling modes measured by the TKI tool, so that you can more easily recognize them. You will learn the primary differences among the five modes and explore common examples of each mode in use.

Then, the booklet will help you use the conflict-handling modes effectively. You will examine the costs and benefits of each mode and get detailed guidelines on when to use and how to skillfully implement each mode.

What Is the TKI® Tool?

The TKI is a self-report questionnaire designed to measure your tendencies in dealing with interpersonal conflict. It describes five different conflict-handling modes and helps you identify which of these modes you use most often. By helping you become more aware of the choices you and others are making in conflict situations, the TKI and its feedback materials provide a way for you to steer conflict situations in constructive directions.

Development of the TKI® Tool

The TKI was developed by Kenneth W. Thomas and Ralph H. Kilmann in the early 1970s. It is based on theoretical refinements by Kenneth Thomas of a model of managerial conflict styles proposed by Robert Blake and Jane Mouton in the 1960s (Blake & Mouton, 1964).

Thomas and Kilmann originally developed the TKI as a research tool. To reduce response bias, they wrote pairs of statements that were carefully matched for desirability, so that no conflict-handling mode sounded better than others. It soon became apparent, however, that the TKI was also a powerful training tool. People liked the idea that each of the modes was desirable in appropriate situations. This idea allowed them not only to appreciate their strengths but also to learn about the value of modes they were using less often.

1

The TKI® Tool Today

In the thirty years since the TKI tool's inception, more than 5 million copies of the instrument have been sold and it has become the leading measure of conflict-handling behavior. It has also been used in hundreds of research studies.

Today the TKI is used in a wide variety of applications, including the following:

- Management and supervisory training
- Negotiation training
- Team building
- Crisis intervention
- Marriage and family counseling

Using This Booklet

If a trainer or facilitator gave you this booklet, it is likely that he or she also gave you some guidance about what to focus on. If not, here are some general suggestions.

- Read through the sections at the beginning of the booklet to make sure you understand and can recognize the five conflict-handling modes.

- If you are part of a team or work group that took the TKI together, be sure to read the material on collaborating. Collaborating on important issues is a key factor in group effectiveness.

Things to Keep in Mind

Here are some useful things to keep in mind as you apply the ideas in this booklet.

Choosing Your Conflict-Handling Modes

- *Remember that you have choices in a conflict.* Be aware that all five conflict-handling modes are available to you. This knowledge gives you a greater sense of control. You can steer conflicts in different directions by choosing different modes.

- *Give yourself time to think.* If you find yourself reacting quickly in a conflict situation, you are probably operating out of old habits. To choose more wisely, slow down your response time. Pause to consider which mode would be most beneficial in this particular situation.

- *Practice applying the guidelines in this booklet.* You won't be able to remember all of them, but some relevant guidelines will come to mind, such as "There's nothing to be gained from raising this issue, so I'll avoid it." Or, "This is important and we might be able to find a win-win solution, so I'll try collaborating." Keep this booklet so that you can brush up occasionally on the guidelines.

Developing New Behavioral Skills

For individuals.

- *Focus on a few new skills at a time.* Pick a few new behaviors that seem most promising, such as saying "and" instead of "but." Concentrate on working them into your behavioral repertoire.

- *Be gentle with yourself.* Skill development goes through predictable cycles, from awkwardness to polish. Don't expect polish right away. Recognize your progress.

- *Continue to add new skills.* As you master new behaviors and they become polished and familiar, you'll have some room to work on adding others. Skim through this booklet occasionally to review your progress and find new skills to try.

For groups.

- *Appoint a monitor.* If your team is going through this training together, choose someone to monitor the group's progress on conflict management.

- *Set group goals.* Establish shared goals in terms of conflict mode use and new skills that the group wants to implement.

- *Review progress periodically.* Agree on a schedule for when the monitor will report to the group (for example, at the end of each meeting, monthly, or quarterly). Have the monitor review the group's progress toward its conflict management goals. Set new goals as appropriate.

What Is Conflict?

onflict is simply *the condition in which people's concerns—the things they care about—appear to be incompatible*. Conflict, then, is something we face every day—a fact of life. Surveys show that managers spend about a quarter of their time handling conflicts. They have to negotiate over resources, handle disagreements over policies, deal with complaints, enforce rules, and manage the inevitable frictions and resentments that occur between people.

Many people make the mistake of equating conflict with fighting—arguing, blaming, name-calling, and so on. This makes conflict seem like a dangerous and destructive thing. However, once you recognize that conflict is simply a condition in which people's concerns appear to be incompatible, it becomes clear that fighting is only one way of dealing with it. This approach allows us to recognize that we have *choices* in how we deal with conflict. It directs our attention to the ways we can control the conflict process through our choices, so that we can manage it constructively. That, of course, is the purpose of the TKI and this booklet.

Two Basic Dimensions of Conflict Behavior

Assertiveness and cooperativeness are the most basic dimensions for describing your choices in a conflict situation. They form the two-dimensional space in which we can locate conflict-handling behaviors, as shown in Figure 1. Note that assertiveness and cooperativeness are separate, independent dimensions. They are *not* opposites of each other.

Assertiveness

Recall that conflict occurs when your concerns appear to be incompatible with someone else's concerns. In that situation, your *assertiveness* is the degree to which you try to satisfy your *own* concerns. This is shown along the vertical axis of the graph in Figure 1. Assertiveness might mean trying to meet your needs or get support for your ideas.

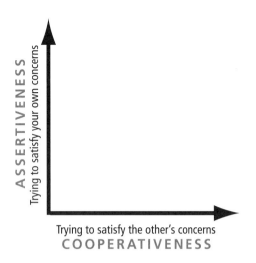

**FIGURE 1 • THE ASSERTIVENESS AND
COOPERATIVENESS DIMENSIONS**

Cooperativeness

Your *cooperativeness* is the degree to which you try to satisfy the *other person's* concerns. This is shown along the horizontal axis of the graph in Figure 1. Cooperativeness might mean helping the other person meet his or her needs or being receptive to the other person's ideas.

What Are the Conflict-Handling Modes?

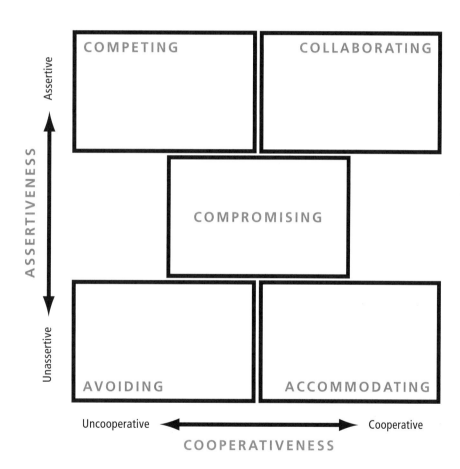

FIGURE 2 • THE FIVE CONFLICT-HANDLING MODES

The conflict-handling modes form the four corners and the center of the two-dimensional space discussed in the preceding section. As shown in Figure 2, they represent the five major combinations of assertiveness and cooperativeness that are possible in a conflict situation.

Competing is assertive and uncooperative. You try to satisfy your own concerns at the other person's expense.

Collaborating is both assertive and cooperative. You try to find a win-win solution that completely satisfies both people's concerns.

5

Compromising is intermediate in both assertiveness and cooperativeness. You try to find an acceptable settlement that only partially satisfies both people's concerns.

Avoiding is both unassertive and uncooperative. You sidestep the conflict without trying to satisfy either person's concerns.

Accommodating is unassertive and cooperative. You attempt to satisfy the other person's concerns at the expense of your own.

Note that these conflict-handling modes are general intentions—your *aims* in a conflict situation—rather than specific *behaviors*. You can use a range of behaviors to enact any conflict-handling mode, depending on the circumstances. For example, you can avoid a conflict by sidestepping an issue, staying out of contact with the other person, or suggesting that you postpone the discussion until a better time. Figure 3 illustrates ways in which each mode can get acted out, helping you recognize the prototypical behaviors associated with each.

COMPETING

Imposing or dictating a decision
"Sorry, Bob, but that's my decision as your supervisor."
Arguing for a conclusion that fits your data
"Our sales show a steady decline. We need to redesign the product."
Hard bargaining (making no concessions)
"I won't take less than $50,000. Take it or leave it."

COLLABORATING

Reconciling interests through a win-win solution
"You need us to fund Project X, but I need Project Y. How can we do both?"
Combining insights into a richer understanding
"You're praising Sally's technical skills, but I'm criticizing her interpersonal difficulties. Both are true, aren't they? She has high potential if she can improve those interpersonal skills."

COMPROMISING

Soft bargaining (exchanging concessions)
"Let's split the difference and settle for $45,000."
Taking turns
"Suppose I pay this time and you pick up the tab next time?"
Moderating your conclusions
"You think he's outstanding, but I think he's average. Suppose we say 'above average'?"

AVOIDING

Avoiding people you find troublesome
"If Fred calls, I'm not in."
Avoiding issues that are unimportant, complex, or dangerous
"Maybe. We'll see. Let's move along to the next topic."
Postponing discussion until later
"Let me check with Accounting and get back to you next week."

ACCOMMODATING

Doing a favor to help someone
"I can see this is important to you. OK."
Being persuaded
"I didn't think of that. You're right."
Obeying an authority
"I'd do it differently, but it's your call."
Deferring to another's expertise
"You're the expert. I'll trust your judgment."
Appeasing someone who is dangerous
"OK, OK. Just calm down."

Assertive

Unassertive

ASSERTIVENESS

Uncooperative ◄─────► Cooperative

COOPERATIVENESS

FIGURE 3 • THE CONFLICT-HANDLING MODES IN ACTION

What Kinds of Tradeoffs Are Involved?

When you choose among the conflict modes, two important dynamics come into play. Briefly, they involve "creating value" and "claiming value" (Lax & Sebenius, 1986). These dynamics involve tradeoffs you must deal with to steer conflict in different directions.

To help us understand these dynamics, we will portray the conflict modes in a somewhat different manner—as ways of dividing up "pies" of satisfaction for the two people involved in a conflict.

Pies of Satisfaction

In Figure 4, circles, or "pies," are used to represent each mode in terms of the amount of satisfaction you intend for both yourself and the other person.

Pieces of the Pie

The size of the *black* area of each pie shown in Figure 4 represents the amount of satisfaction you are seeking for your *own* concerns—that is, how much of the pie you're after for yourself. Notice that as you move upward in the figure, the more assertive modes show larger black areas—since you use them to try to satisfy your own concerns more completely.

The *gray* area of each pie represents the amount of satisfaction you intend for the *other* person. Notice that as you move to the right in the figure, the more cooperative modes show larger gray areas—since you use them to try to satisfy the other person's concerns more fully.

Sizes of the Pies

The overall size of each pie in Figure 4 represents the amount of joint satisfaction you intend for both people—that is, the total of the satisfaction you intend for your concerns and for the other person's concerns. Notice that the pies are of three different sizes. Figure 5 shows how the conflict-handling modes relate to the three sizes of pie—labeled lose-lose, win-lose, and win-win.

- With avoiding, the pie is very small or nonexistent. Avoiding is sometimes called *lose-lose* because it pursues no immediate satisfaction for either person. The conflict issue is not addressed, so neither person's concerns are satisfied.

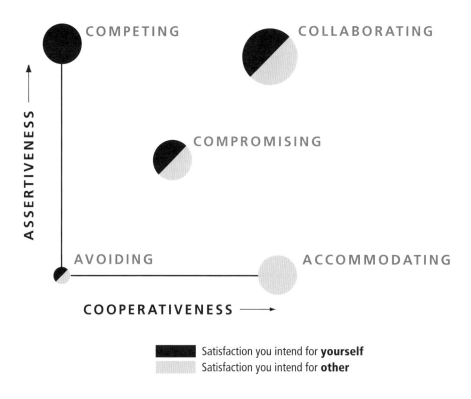

FIGURE 4 • PIES OF SATISFACTION

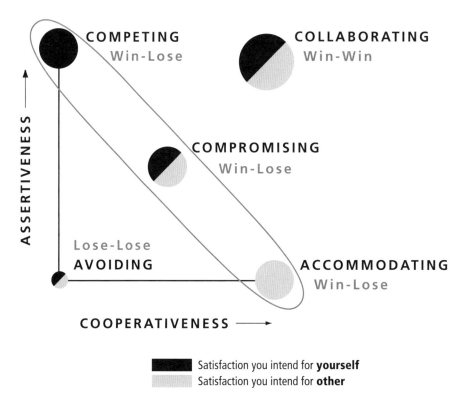

FIGURE 5 • THREE SIZES OF PIE: LOSE-LOSE, WIN-LOSE, AND WIN-WIN

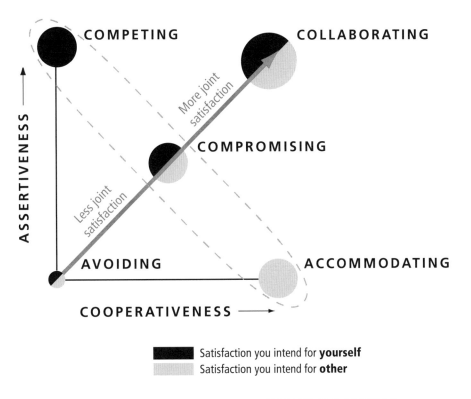

FIGURE 6 • CREATING VALUE: INCREASING THE SIZE OF THE PIE

Creating Value: Increasing the Size of the Pie

One set of conflict dynamics, then, involves deciding how much joint satisfaction you will try to attain—that is, how large a pie you're intending. The process of creating more joint satisfaction is often called "creating value." You try to create more value as you move from lose-lose to win-lose to win-win in the model, along the diagonal pointing northeast, as shown in Figure 6.

Creating value requires committing one's time and psychological energy to facing the conflict and digging into the conflict issue. When you decide to create more value, then, you are deciding to *invest* more time and energy in the conflict issue.

■ With competing, compromising and accommodating, the pie is larger but still only big enough to fully satisfy one person (or to partially satisfy both people). These modes are often called *win-lose*. As different as these three modes appear to be, they share an important distinction: they all allow for a limited amount of possible satisfaction. One person's gains become the other person's losses.

■ With collaborating, the pie is still larger—large enough to fully satisfy both people's concerns. Collaborating is often called *win-win*. It is an attempt to *expand* the pie so that it is large enough to satisfy the concerns of both people.

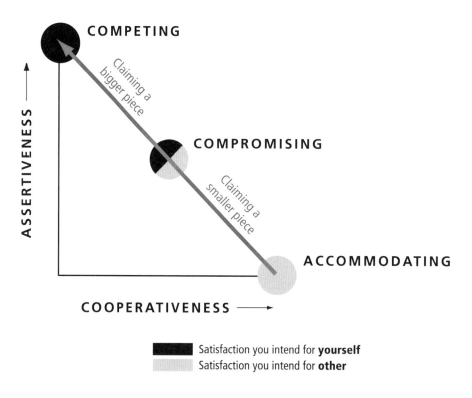

FIGURE 7 • CLAIMING VALUE: TAKING MORE OF A LIMITED PIE

■ When you **avoid** a conflict issue, you are deciding to save your time and energy for other matters, creating no value on that conflict issue.

■ When you adopt one of the win-lose modes—that is, when you **compete, accommodate,** or **compromise**—you are deciding to invest some time and energy in the conflict in order to create some limited value. You invest the time and energy needed to surface and settle the conflict issue, but you don't dig very deeply into the underlying issue. You take the apparent incompatibility of people's stated positions at face value: "I want us to do X, but you want us to do Y." So you are forced to pursue X (compete), allow the other person to get Y (accommodate), or settle for half X and half Y (compromise).

■ When you **collaborate,** you are deciding not only to surface the conflict but also to dig more deeply into the conflict issue. You invest this extra time and energy in the hope of creating added value. You try to identify the concerns underlying your position and the other's position in such a way that you can find a win-win solution that completely satisfies both parties. "I'm pushing for this new product, while you're opposing it. You seem to care mostly about conserving our cash, while I care about expanding our product line. Is there a way we can do both—maybe think up some new products that wouldn't cost much to develop?"

Claiming Value: Taking More of a Limited Pie

The other set of dynamics comes into play when you have defined the conflict in win-lose terms: "I want X, but you want Y." It involves deciding how much of the limited pie you will try to get for yourself. This process is often called "claiming value." You claim greater value when you move from accommodating to compromising to competing along the diagonal pointing northwest, as shown in Figure 7.

By definition, claiming value, a win-lose activity, occurs at the expense of the other person. For that reason, the more value you claim, the greater the resistance you can expect, and the greater the strain you put on your relationship with the other person. In many ways, then, the decision to claim more value involves deciding how much to risk both the other's cooperation and his or her goodwill in attempting to more fully satisfy your concerns.

You can also think of claiming value in terms of giving and taking.

- **Accommodating** is about giving. You give up your claim to the pie so that the other person's concerns can be fully satisfied. In win-lose terms, you lose, allowing the other to win. Rather than risk the relationship, you maintain or build goodwill by helping the other.

- **Compromising** is about both giving and taking. You hold out for only half of the pie, putting only a modest strain on your relationship. You give up some satisfaction of your concerns to take some partial satisfaction. You "split the difference" so that there is no clear winner or loser, but rather a combination of gains and losses for each.

- **Competing** is about taking—claiming all of the limited value. You decide to risk more sizeable resistance and damage to your relationship in order to prevail. You try to completely satisfy your own concerns at the expense of the other person's concerns. You are trying to win.

What Is the Best Way to Handle Conflict?

There is no single best way to handle conflict. Each of the five conflict-handling modes has costs and benefits. Each can be highly effective when used in the right circumstances and when applied skillfully.

Your effectiveness in handling conflict, then, depends on two factors:

- Knowing *when* to use each mode
- Having the *skills* to perform each mode well

Your skills, in turn, can also be broken down into two components:

- Being able to *realize the benefits* of a mode (for example, being able to win your position when competing)
- Being able to *minimize the costs* of that mode (for example, competing without damaging relationships and provoking anger)

The rest of this booklet provides information you will need to address these issues. Figures 8 and 9 show the benefits and the costs of the five modes. This material is followed by a section of detailed guidance on when and how to use each mode most effectively.

BENEFITS

COMPETING

Asserting your position
Standing up for your interests and ideas; making sure they are taken seriously

Possibility of quick victory
Making a quick recommendation; pressing for a quick decision if you have enough power to prevail

Self-defense
Protecting your interests and views from attack

Testing assumptions
Debating to expose and test your own and others' assumptions

COLLABORATING

High-quality decisions
Seeking innovative solutions that are better than each person's recommendations ("synergy")

Learning and communication
Exchanging information openly, aiding communication and discovery

Resolution and commitment
Working toward meeting both people's concerns fully so that conflict is resolved and people are committed to the decision

Strengthening relationships
Building respect, liking, and trust; resolving problems in a relationship

COMPROMISING

Pragmatism
Practicing "the art of the possible"; getting a deal that's good enough

Speed and expediency
Making expedient settlements

Fairness
Providing equal gains and losses for both people

Maintaining relationships
Meeting halfway to reduce the strain on relationships

ASSERTIVENESS

Assertive

Unassertive

AVOIDING

Reducing stress
Avoiding demanding or unpleasant people and topics

Saving time
Not wasting time and energy on low-priority issues

Steering clear of danger
Not stirring up a hornet's nest or provoking trouble

Setting up more favorable conditions
Gaining time to be better prepared, less distracted

ACCOMMODATING

Helping someone out
Helping people meet their needs; supporting them

Restoring harmony
Smoothing feathers; calming troubled waters

Building relationships
Building social capital by doing favors, helping; apologizing when necessary

Choosing a quick ending
Cutting your losses so you can move on

Uncooperative ◄————————► Cooperative

COOPERATIVENESS

FIGURE 8 • BENEFITS ASSOCIATED WITH EACH CONFLICT-HANDLING MODE

COSTS

COMPETING

Strained work relationships
Losers feel resentful, exploited

Suboptimal decisions
Possible win-win solutions are overlooked; information is not exchanged freely

Decreased initiative and motivation
When decisions are imposed, others are less committed to them, show less initiative and motivation

Possible escalation and deadlock
If initial tactics fail, temptation is to use more extreme, provocative tactics; negotiations may deadlock

COLLABORATING

Time and energy required
More time is needed to dig through issues; full concentration and creativity are required

Psychological demands
Requires openness to new viewpoints, ideas, and challenges; can be psychologically demanding

Possibility of offending
May involve working through sensitive issues; can make things worse and hurt feelings if unsuccessful

Vulnerability risk
Others may try to exploit your openness and flexibility

COMPROMISING

Partially sacrificed concerns
Both people's concerns are compromised, leaving some residual frustration; issue isn't fully resolved, may flare up again

Suboptimal solutions
Compromise decisions are less innovative and of lower quality than successful collaborative decisions

Superficial understandings
Agreements often paper over differences with vague statements that don't accurately reflect the beliefs of the people who disagree

AVOIDING

Declining working relationships
Work may not get accomplished if people avoid each other; hostile stereotypes are allowed to develop and fester

Resentment
Others whose concerns are being neglected may resent your avoiding, see it as evasive

Delays
Unaddressed issues cause delays, may keep recurring—taking up more time and causing more frustration than if faced earlier

Degraded communication and decision making
People may walk on eggshells rather than speaking candidly and learning from each other

ACCOMMODATING

Sacrificed concerns
Something you care about is conceded—your interests or your views are sacrificed

Loss of respect
Although cooperativeness can build goodwill, low assertiveness can lose you respect; a pattern of accommodating can encourage exploitation by others

Loss of motivation
More accommodating means less satisfaction; you may find yourself agreeing to things for which you have little enthusiasm

ASSERTIVENESS — Assertive / Unassertive

Uncooperative ←——————→ Cooperative

COOPERATIVENESS

FIGURE 9 • COSTS ASSOCIATED WITH EACH CONFLICT-HANDLING MODE

How Can I Use Each Mode Most Effectively?

The remainder of this booklet provides detailed guidance to help you make two sets of informed choices for each mode: when to use it and how to skillfully implement it.

Deciding When to Use a Mode

As seen in the previous section, each conflict-handling mode has benefits and costs associated with it. The relative weights of those benefits and costs depend on the situation. This section will spell out situations in which the benefits of each mode are especially valuable and other situations in which the costs of that mode are least acceptable. There are situations, then, when each mode is clearly more appropriate than the others.

Behavioral Skills

Each conflict-handling mode is an intention that can be enacted in different ways—through different behaviors. It follows, then, that there are specific behaviors—or skills—that are more likely to realize that mode's benefits and minimize its costs.

People who are less skilled at managing conflict often accept the costs of different modes as inevitable. For example, they may rationalize that "you have to break some eggs to make an omelet." However, there are learnable skills that can help reduce the costs of each mode. Examples include avoiding an issue without appearing evasive, compromising and accommodating without appearing weak, and competing without provoking anger.

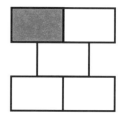

COMPETING

RECAPPING THE BASICS

Competing occurs when you take a position that would satisfy your concerns but not the other person's, and you try to prevail. It is a win-lose mode in which you use some form of power to win your position, often against the resistance of the other person.

Common examples
- Imposing or dictating a decision
- Arguing for a conclusion that fits your data
- Hard bargaining (making no concessions)

Benefits
- Asserting your position
- Possibility of quick victory
- Self-defense
- Testing assumptions

Costs
- Strained work relationships
- Suboptimal decisions
- Decreased initiative and motivation
- Possible escalation and deadlock

Deciding When to Compete

- Use competing sparingly
- Compete on vital issues where collaborating isn't feasible

Use Competing Sparingly

Competing has strong effects and should not be over-used. Although it is necessary and useful in many situations, it can impose significant costs on relationships, decision making, and motivation. In its escalated forms, it is particularly destructive. People are sensitive to competing behavior, and a few examples can be enough for them to form negative opinions.

Compete on Vital Issues Where Collaborating Isn't Feasible

In conflicts over very important issues, you will generally want to use the two most assertive modes, competing and collaborating, to try to fully satisfy your concerns. Collaborating does not incur most of the costs of competing and produces superior win-win solutions when successful, so it is usually preferable. Restrict your competing to high-stakes conflicts where collaborating is *not* feasible.

When you know you're right.

There are times when you will see issues more clearly than others will. You may have more experience or information, or you may be less influenced by vested interests or other biases. When these issues are crucial to the organization's welfare but you encounter resistance from others, the organization needs for you to argue your position as persuasively as you can.

When unpopular actions need to be taken.

Managers sometimes have to take actions that appear harmful to the interests of specific individuals. Examples include terminations, budget cuts, and disciplinary actions. It is rare for a person affected by these actions to support them, so there is often resistance. Use firmness to impose these decisions if necessary.

When quick, decisive action is required.

In a crisis situation such as an emergency rescue, there is often no time for a collaborative discussion. Someone with authority or expertise needs to take control and issue directions.

When you're under attack.

When you are being attacked and the stakes are high, you need to defend yourself. If someone unfairly attacks the competence of your department during a meeting, for example, it is important to challenge that view—to prevent its being believed by the rest of the organization.

When consensus fails.

Research shows that effective management groups prefer a collaborative, consensus-seeking approach to important issues. However, when it becomes clear that consensus can't be reached, they give the decision to the people with the greatest authority over the issue. Those people impose a decision that takes the group's input into account. This saves time and prevents the disagreeing parties from becoming entrenched in escalated, competitive debates.

When people are too considerate.

When groups are very cohesive, people may accommodate one another out of politeness, producing "groupthink." To prevent this, cohesive groups sometimes use controlled forms of competing on key issues. For instance, two people can be assigned to argue different positions in a structured debate, or a devil's advocate can be appointed to challenge the group's preferred position.

Behavioral Skills for Competing

- Being persuasive
- Fighting fair
- Using warnings instead of threats
- Imposing a decision
- Using tough love to enforce standards

Being Persuasive

When you compete, you rely on power to get others to accept your position. There are many different kinds of power you can use, with different side effects. As a rule of thumb, try persuasion first. When persuasion is successful, others won't simply comply with your position—they will be convinced of its merits and committed to its implementation.

Lay the groundwork.

Your persuasiveness depends partly on the information you can muster to make your case and partly on your relationship with other people. Others are more likely to be persuaded when they respect your credibility and feel goodwill toward you. For that reason, do what you can to build credibility and goodwill in your organization—in addition to doing your homework on important issues.

Explain your motives.

It is easy for people to misread your aims when you compete. They may mistakenly believe that you are on a power trip, have a hidden agenda, are mad at them, or are opposed to their concerns. These misperceptions will lead the people who hold them to discount what you say, so be sure to briefly spell out your motives. If you can anticipate how others might misread your motives, try to head off those interpretations: "I usually agree with Fred, and I'm sympathetic to the needs of the Accounting Department, but I am really concerned that this proposal would reduce our firm's competitiveness." "Susan, I don't mean to be critical, but I have some feedback that may help you meet your production goals."

Appeal to shared concerns.

When you're trying to persuade others that your position is "best," you need to appeal to shared notions of what is important—for example, the organization's mission, shared ethical standards, or the welfare of the organization's members. Show how your position would contribute to these shared concerns: "The engineers tell me this machine will double our production, and George in Accounting assures me it'll pay for itself within six months." "Two of my best performers have told me they're considering leaving if we don't provide more training. It seems to be time for us to increase our training allowances."

Be specific and credible.

In a heated discussion, you may be tempted to strengthen your position by exaggerating. Doing so is likely to undermine your credibility on this and future issues. Do your homework, stick to the evidence, and be honest about its certainty or reliability: "Gwen tells me Acme is forming a new division aimed at our market. I haven't been able to confirm that yet, but it would be a serious threat to us if it's true. I think Bob and I should investigate this and, if it *is* true, begin to plan a counterstrategy." "Our turnover rate is up by 15 percent so far this year, and grievances are up 30 percent. I think it's likely that we *do* have a morale problem in this department, so I think we should hire this consulting firm to find out why."

Fighting Fair

Rules of fairness keep competing within limits so that it doesn't escalate and become destructive. They also make it more likely that a good decision will be reached. When you fight fair, then, you are more likely

to maintain your goodwill and credibility and to serve the larger interests of your organization.

Stick to the current issue.

It is often tempting, in the midst of a discussion, to bring up conflict issues other than the one at hand. You may be tempted to bring up instances in the past when the other person was wrong or to air old grievances: "And while we're on the subject, how about the time you . . . !" Bringing up these old issues "muddies the water"; issues proliferate so that it becomes difficult to reach a decision. These issues may also inject old emotional conflicts into the discussion. So try to keep your discussion focused on the issue at hand. (See "Avoid Emotional Conflicts," on page 34, and "Breaking the Anger Cycle," on pages 36–37.)

Be respectful.

Don't let impatience turn into rudeness, sarcasm, or other demeaning behavior. Remind yourself that you want to create allies rather than enemies and to build a collegial climate. Rudeness and sarcasm are forms of bullying behavior that won't help you achieve those goals. If you tend to use words like *silly, crazy,* and *stupid* to describe other people's comments, replace them with less evaluative comments like "I don't see your logic there," "That doesn't follow from the data," or "I don't think that would work." (See "Breaking the Anger Cycle," on pages 36–37.)

Listen and respond.

People also feel bullied when you don't let them express their views or don't take them seriously. For example, you may interrupt others when they try to talk or talk over their comments in a louder voice. You may also ignore what they say or make light of their views, so that you don't respond to their points. These tactics may occasionally help you win an argument, but they won't produce good decisions or goodwill. So try to give the other person a fair opportunity to express his or her views, listen, and respond to what has actually been said.

Act as a referee for others.

It's not enough just to strive to be fair yourself. You'll also want to help set and enforce rules of fairness in the conflict behavior of others. In a conflict between two members of a committee, for example, the other members can serve as referees to enforce fairness standards and establish them as constructive norms: "You're not letting Sally finish her point, Carl." "I don't think that's what Tony said." "Can we keep personalities out of this?" "I think it will be more helpful if you try to make your point without the sarcasm." It may take active involvement by several people to stop severe cases of bullying.

Using Warnings Instead of Threats

As a form of power, punishment is usually a last resort and needs to be used with care. It tends to produce resistance and destroy goodwill. Threats of punishment can also escalate a conflict by provoking counterthreats and reprisals. Still, there are times when you will need to remind people that you can do punishing things to them—such as terminating a poor performer's employment, giving a negative performance evaluation, or canceling a contract. How can you do this in a way that is constructive?

Don't threaten.

A *threat* is a promise to do something punishing if another person doesn't comply with one's wishes. The punishment is something that would cost the person making the threat and that he or she would prefer not to have to do. For example, someone might threaten, "If you don't promote Jim, I'll quit." But if he did quit, he'd be out of a job in a tight market—a risk he would rather not take.

Threats have a number of drawbacks. They appear hostile, seeming to be directed against other people and their interests. They also seem arbitrary and unfair. There is no apparent reason for the threat except to prevail—to coerce the other person. Finally, they often lack credibility. Because enforcing the threat doesn't appear to be in your interest, there is a question of whether you may be bluffing. If the other person concludes that you are bluffing and calls you on it, you are forced to choose between two undesirable options—giving in (and being caught in the bluff) or having to follow through on something that's not in your best interest. Either way, you lose something.

Use warnings.

In contrast, a *warning* is a statement about what you will have to do (and what would be in your interest to do) if the person does not do what you advise. "If I don't get more resources and qualified people, this division won't survive for long. If I see that happening, it won't be in my best interest to stay. It would be like having 'Captain of the *Titanic*' on my resume."

Warnings have a different feel than threats. They seem more reasonable and less arbitrary. They provide a reason why something would have to be done. Rather than being hostile, they have the flavor of giving the other some useful information that helps him or her make a better decision—of helping the other person avoid a mistake. Because they provide an explanation of why your action would be necessary, warnings also appear more credible than threats.

Imposing a Decision

To impose a decision when you are in a leadership position and persuasion doesn't work, you need to marshal the power that comes with your position. As an example, imagine that you are the CEO of an organization whose division presidents are very busy, stretched to their limits. After studying the matter, you realize that divisional information systems need to be redesigned. You've discussed this with the division presidents, but they resist because of the extra work required. Your next steps are as follows.

Assert your authority.

Make sure people understand your reasoning. It often helps to express regret that they don't agree and empathize with the extra work your decision will entail, but remind them that it is your decision to make: "This is my call and my responsibility." Signal that the discussion phase is over, and it is now time to act: "Sorry, Jessica, but the decision has been made."

Reward the new behavior.

Use the reward system to create incentives for the new behavior and to signal its importance to performance. The purpose is not to bribe people to go along with you, but to reward what you see as contributing to the organization's mission. Build your decision into job descriptions, performance appraisal criteria, and the incentive system as appropriate. Collect information on people's implementation of the decision as part of performance appraisal.

Follow up on deviations.

If people appear not to be implementing the decision, find out why. Offer to provide needed help if there are problems. If the reasons aren't convincing, remind people that you see the decision as vital for the organization and ask for an implementation plan. If the plan isn't developed or followed, issue warnings. Carry through on the warnings if needed. Use "tough love" (see below).

Using Tough Love to Enforce Standards

Enforcing standards is one of the most sensitive and difficult parts of leadership. Many managers fall into the mental trap of choosing between "hardness" and "softness" in dealing with these situations. To be soft is to be so considerate that standards may not be enforced. To be hard means taking a firm stand and being so quick to punish that team members feel the leader is playing "gotcha" rather than supporting them. Research suggests an approach called "tough love," which avoids these pitfalls.

Be supportive.

When you meet with a person to discuss a standard that isn't being met, make it clear that you are concerned about his or her welfare. Your purpose in the meeting is to see if you can find a way to help

him or her succeed. (This is the "love" part of tough love.) Offer any counseling that would help the person develop a plan to meet the standard. Provide any resources you can to help him or her succeed, such as additional training or short-term help.

Be tough-minded.

The toughness in tough love involves squarely facing the fact that important standards are not being met. It is usually a mistake to blur this reality out of concern for the other person's feelings. The person needs this information to make good decisions, and the organization needs to have the standards met. Ask if the person understands the importance of the standards to the organization's mission. Make sure he or she realizes that the standards are not being met, the size of the shortfall, and that you cannot allow those unmet standards to continue. Warn the person about deadlines and consequences. Document your discussion according to the personnel requirements of your organization.

Raise the issue of "fit."

If it looks as if the person will continue to fall short of the standard or seems unwilling to comply, raise the issue of the person's fit with the job: "Are you happy in this job?" "Do you really want to be here?" If there is a poor fit, you will be doing both the organization and the person a favor by helping the person find a better one. If you feel there might be a good fit elsewhere in the organization, help the person find it. If not, offer whatever resources the organization provides to help the person find it outside.

SUMMARY: WHEN AND HOW TO COMPETE

DECIDING WHEN TO COMPETE

Use competing sparingly

Compete on vital issues where collaborating isn't feasible
- When you know you're right
- When unpopular actions need to be taken
- When quick, decisive action is required
- When you're under attack
- When consensus fails
- When people are too considerate

BEHAVIORAL SKILLS FOR COMPETING

Being persuasive
- Lay the groundwork
- Explain your motives
- Appeal to shared concerns
- Be specific and credible

Fighting fair
- Stick to the current issue
- Be respectful
- Listen and respond
- Act as a referee for others

Using warnings instead of threats
- Don't threaten
- Use warnings

Imposing a decision
- Assert your authority
- Reward the new behavior
- Follow up on deviations

Using tough love to enforce standards
- Be supportive
- Be tough-minded
- Raise the issue of "fit"

COLLABORATING

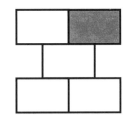

RECAPPING THE BASICS

Collaborating occurs when you try to find a position that would fully satisfy your own and the other person's concerns. It is a win-win mode that moves you toward an integrative solution.

Common examples

- Reconciling interests through a win-win solution
- Combining insights into a richer understanding

Benefits

- High-quality decisions
- Learning and communication
- Resolution and commitment
- Strengthening relationships

Costs

- Time and energy required
- Psychological demands
- Possibility of offending
- Vulnerability risk

Deciding When to Collaborate

- Recognize (and build) the conditions that enable collaboration
- Try to collaborate on important issues

Recognize (and Build) the Conditions That Enable Collaboration

Collaborating is feasible only when the following elements are present in sufficient amounts. Don't invest your time in collaborating when any one of them is missing.

- Time
- Interpersonal skills
- Integrative possibilities in the issue
- Trust
- Openness to new ideas

Because collaborative solutions are often desirable, however, do what you can to build collaboration-enabling conditions over the longer term. Help build these conditions by

- Setting aside time to study important issues
- Providing training in conflict management skills
- Identifying promising win-win issues to explore
- Building trust and goodwill
- Fostering a climate of discovery and openness to new ideas

Try to Collaborate on Important Issues

When collaborating is feasible, use it on *important* issues. When an issue is significant but not important, compromising will produce a good enough outcome. But on more important issues, the added benefit of a win-win outcome is usually worth the extra time you will need to invest. Collaborating is especially desirable or necessary in the following situations.

When both concerns are vital to an organization.

In the transportation industry, for example, many conflicts arise around meeting schedule commitments versus ensuring safety. It is vital to find ways of doing both without compromising either. In manufacturing organizations, the same is true for issues of quality versus cost. Finding innovative, win-win solutions in these conflicts allows organizations to prosper and gives them a comparative advantage.

When you want to learn.

Collaborative discussions are the most straightforward means of learning from others. They allow you to test your assumptions, explore different ways of looking at issues, and take in new information: "That's interesting. Why do you say that? I've been thinking about it this way . . . What do you think?"

Competitive arguments are less efficient for learning because energy gets channeled into defending your existing views. Studies show that innovative scientists, for example, tend to be more collaborative than competitive.

To merge insights from diverse perspectives.

When decisions need to be made about complex issues, you need to involve people who are knowledgeable about different aspects of the issues. Most decision

groups, then—whether boards of directors, project teams, executive committees, or ad hoc committees—include people with diverse perspectives and areas of expertise. This diversity is challenging to manage because it introduces conflicting insights. However, collaborating provides a way of "harvesting" a more complete understanding from the diversity.

When a top management team considers introducing a new product, for example, a marketing manager may see the opportunity to grab new markets and support the move—while a financial officer may see the cash flow threat and argue against it. In a collaborative setting, the team can integrate these insights to see a significant marketing opportunity with some cash flow risks. It can then explore ways of capitalizing on the opportunity and managing the risks.

When you need commitment to a decision.

In a group setting, collaborative decision processes—such as decision by consensus—give people a chance to incorporate their most important concerns into a decision, along with their suggestions. For that reason, group members feel more committed to collaborative decisions than to compromises or accommodations. Engage people in collaborative decision making, then, when commitment is important to carrying out a decision and cannot be taken for granted.

To work through problems in a relationship.

Over time, unresolved issues can build up hard feelings in a relationship as frustrations accumulate from past compromises and accommodations. Collaborating provides a way to surface and resolve core problems in the relationship: "The truth is, I really don't like it when you interrupt me and change the topic." "I can appreciate that, but sometimes you seem to wander from the point and I get impatient." "Suppose you just tell me briefly when you think I'm off the point?" "OK, I'll try that."

Behavioral Skills for Collaborating

- Setting the right tone when raising the issue
- Identifying both people's underlying concerns
- Stating the conflict as a mutual problem
- Brainstorming solutions and picking the best one
- Being firm when necessary: "firm flexibility"
- Collaborating in groups

Setting the Right Tone When Raising the Issue

If you don't surface the conflict issue, you will remain in a lose-lose, avoiding mode. When you raise the issue, do it in a way that doesn't seem competitive or create defensiveness.

Picture the other person's positive concerns.

In conflicts it is easy to misread others' intentions and assume that they are simply making trouble for you. Before you raise an issue, stop to identify the *positive* concerns the other person is probably pursuing. This gives you a head start at problem solving and gets you into a more constructive frame of mind.

Use "we" language and avoid assigning blame.

When you raise the issue, talk about the shared problem you're having: "It seems we are having trouble agreeing on these procedures." "Our scheduling has been causing us problems, hasn't it?" Don't blame the problem on the other person. It will only set up defensiveness and make collaborating difficult. (See "Avoid Emotional Conflicts," on page 34.)

Mention the benefits of a solution.

Spell out the positive outcomes you both can achieve by solving the problem: "I'm hoping we can work out a solution to get this project moving faster." Mention the specific concerns you think the other person has: "I'm hoping we can improve quality as well as speed up the process."

Ask if this is a good time.

You may be ready and eager to raise the issue, but you'll also need to respect the other person's schedule and give him or her a chance to prepare. Set up a time and setting that works for both of you. (See "Know When to Postpone an Issue," on pages 34–35.)

Identifying Both People's Underlying Concerns

This is the single most important step in collaborating—an absolute necessity for getting beyond win-lose dynamics.

Recognize the difference between concerns and positions.

Collaborating requires that you focus on underlying concerns rather than positions. Here is an example to illustrate the difference.

> Fred is an accountant with a medium-sized firm. He receives a purchase order from a senior executive, Susan, who wants to spend some of her funds on a party for her successful product development team. However, Fred knows that accounting policies won't allow this pot of money to be spent on a party.

A **concern** is *the thing a person cares about* in the conflict—the thing that appears to be threatened. In this example, Fred's concern is that the company's fiscal rules be followed, while Susan's concern is that her team's accomplishment be celebrated. In contrast, a **position** is *an action you propose* to settle the conflict—what you think should be done. In this example, Fred could take any of a number of different positions: that Susan's request should be denied, that this exception should be allowed, and so on.

Don't jump to positions.

Win-lose conflicts are usually disagreements over positions: either you or the other person takes a position about what should be done ("we should do X") and then the other disagrees ("no, we should not do X"). When conflict is framed in terms of positions (whether or not to do X), it is impossible to find a win-win outcome. You can do X (you win, the other loses), not do X (you lose, the other wins), or do X partway (a compromise). Those are the only logical possibilities.

In the above example, Fred and Susan will not be able to collaborate if they define the conflict issue as whether or not Susan can spend her funds on a party. The only possibilities are win-lose: fund the party (Susan wins, Fred loses), don't fund the party (Fred wins, Susan loses), or fund a smaller party (both compromise).

In collaborating, then, don't jump to positions. Delay discussing "what we should do" until both of you have identified what you want to achieve—your concerns. "Let's hold off talking about what we should do until we both understand what we need."

Clarify and share your underlying concern.

Often you have to stop to figure out what you care about in a conflict situation that is pulling you and the other person in different directions: "Look, what's most important to me is that this project comes in on time. I'm concerned that if we change its scope now we may miss the deadline." "I guess the reason I'd like that assignment is that it would give me the opportunity to learn something new. I'm concerned that I'll stagnate if I keep doing the same old thing."

Help clarify the other person's underlying concern.

Ask the other person what his or her concern is: "What's most important to you here?" If the person answers in terms of a position ("I want us to do X"), ask *why* he or she wants that to happen. Don't make this sound like a cross-examination. You are trying to find a way to meet the person's concern, not to expose holes in his or her reasoning.

If the other person is struggling to express his or her concerns, use active listening skills: "So you're saying you want a project that will let you learn more about avionics. Do I have that right?" "It sounds like you are worried that this new product will be hard to market. Is that right?"

Stating the Conflict as a Mutual Problem

Once you are clear about both people's underlying concerns, you can state the conflict issue in a way that invites a win-win solution.

Say "and" rather than "but."

Lay the groundwork for an integrative solution by describing your concern and the other person's in ways that don't sound incompatible. Rather than say, "I want X, *but* you want Y," try saying, "I want X, *and* you want Y." The difference between "but" and "and" is profound.

In the case of Fred and Susan, for example, Fred might say, "Let's see. You want a party for your team and I need to follow our accounting rules." As is usually the case when you get down to underlying concerns, there is no basic incompatibility.

State the integrative problem: How can we do both?

Here, you explicitly frame the conflict issue as a shared problem to be solved: "Is there a way we can meet both our concerns?" "Both of those things are important. How can we do both?" In this step, you enlist the other person as an *ally*. There is a shift in atmosphere that often shows up in seating arrangements: you may move from being possible adversaries sizing each other up across the table to colleagues sitting next to each other looking at the same notes and sketches.

In the case of Fred and Susan, Susan might ask, "So, how can we find a way to fund a party without breaking the rules?" Or Fred might say, "Let's see if we can find another way to pay for your party." At this point, Susan becomes a customer to Fred rather than a possible rule violator, and Fred becomes a resource to Susan rather than a bureaucratic obstacle.

Brainstorming Solutions and Picking the Best One

Now the two of you try to think of actions that would satisfy both your concerns.

Stay flexible.

As you problem solve, don't quickly latch on to an action as your preferred position. Stay open to new ways of meeting your concern and encourage the other person to do the same: "That idea is promising, but let's see if we can find an even better one."

For example, suppose Fred says, "The real problem is using your project funds. It's because it's a government project that you can't fund a party. I know your division has other funds. Ask your vice president if he's willing to fund the party." Susan might say, "I'll think about that, but are there other ways to do this?"

Use tentative, exploratory language.

One way to stay flexible is to not use overly certain phrases such as "we need to . . ." and "we should . . ." The creative part of problem solving requires that you be able to try out ideas, so it helps to use phrases such as "suppose we . . . ?" and "what would happen if we . . . ?"

Fred, for example, might ask, "Suppose your celebration wasn't a party, so that you didn't serve booze or invite spouses? Suppose you had a special team meeting to review your progress? You could still celebrate and could even hand out booklets or a video on the project." "That's an idea. I could even hand out plaques, right?" "Sure."

Agree on the best solution.

Once you have identified a number of possible solutions, pick the one that works best for both of you. It should be comparatively easy to agree on one of these solutions, since all of them are intended to satisfy your concerns.

Susan: "I think I'll go with the special meeting. That way, I won't have to ask for extra funds." Fred: "Great."

Being Firm When Necessary: "Firm Flexibility"

Collaborating is easiest when the other person is also in a collaborative state of mind. It is more challenging when the other person is competing—pushing a position that would not satisfy your concerns. This situation requires you to be more firm. For example, consider the following example.

> Karen, the operations manager of a shipping firm, walks into the maintenance supervisor's office and says, "Bill, I hear you sidelined our big rig for maintenance. I need you to release it for a trip on Thursday." Bill responds, "Wait a minute. That truck isn't safe. It's past its mileage threshold and is due for a major overhaul." Not listening, Karen pushes her position: "That truck was making deliveries last week, and now it's not safe? Come on, I need it for one more delivery. The customer is really screaming."

When you (like Bill) face this situation, remember what you need to be firm about. Be firm (assertive) about any important concerns you have. At the same time, stay flexible about your position so you can look for collaborative solutions. This stance is called "firm flexibility" (Pruitt & Rubin, 1986). Show the other person that you are firmly committed to satisfying your concern, so that you can't accept his or her position, but also indicate your willingness to help find another solution.

> Bill responds to Karen, "That truck is unsafe. The last driver reported brake problems. I won't send out an unsafe truck. But let's see if we can figure out a way to get your load delivered safely." Depending on Karen's need and the problems with the truck, they may find a number of possible solutions: for example, delivering the load in two smaller trucks, fixing the safety problems on this truck before Thursday (and delaying the rest of the overhaul until after the delivery), or authorizing overtime expenses to get the entire overhaul completed before Thursday.

Collaborating in Groups

A study of effective top management teams found that the following tactics promoted effective collaboration in group settings (Eisenhardt, Kahwajy, & Burgeois, 1997).

Work with more, rather than less, information.

Providing the group with lots of up-to-date, objective data helps with accurate problem solving. It also keeps the group from arguing over uninformed speculations and preconceptions.

Develop multiple alternatives.

When there are only one or two options, groups tend to take sides and get into competitive arguments. Developing multiple options gives the group a richer set to consider and makes it easier for group members to change their minds. Creating new alternatives is also fun and helps build cohesiveness.

Create common goals.

Shared goals are powerful devices for building cohesiveness and collaboration. Create a common goal for group members to rally around. Make sure people see their role as achieving that goal, rather than representing their departments' interests.

Use humor.

Humor creates a positive mood in a group, which in turn makes people more open-minded, creative, and nondefensive. Humor also allows group members to say things in a way that gets around others' defenses. (See "Use humor to defuse tension," on page 37.)

Balance the power structure.

Collaborating is easiest when the leader plays an active role and also involves group members in the discussion. In contrast, weak leaders create power vacuums that spawn competitive politics, while autocratic leaders suppress collaborative inputs from other members.

Seek consensus with qualification.

Collaborating is best enacted through consensual decision making. All group members have a chance to air their concerns, suggest alternatives, and state their reasons for supporting an alternative. However, when consensus fails, forcing the group to keep trying to reach agreement can lead to endless haggling. Under consensus with qualification, the most relevant senior manager will then make the decision, guided by inputs other group members have made.

SUMMARY: WHEN AND HOW TO COLLABORATE

DECIDING WHEN TO COLLABORATE	*BEHAVIORAL SKILLS FOR COLLABORATING*

Recognize (and build) the conditions that enable collaboration

Try to collaborate on important issues
- When both concerns are vital to an organization
- When you want to learn
- To merge insights from diverse perspectives
- When you need commitment to a decision
- To work through problems in a relationship

Setting the right tone when raising the issue
- Picture the other person's positive concerns
- Use "we" language and avoid assigning blame
- Mention the benefits of a solution
- Ask if this is a good time

Identifying both people's underlying concerns
- Recognize the difference between concerns and positions
- Don't jump to positions
- Clarify and share your underlying concern
- Help clarify the other person's underlying concern

Stating the conflict as a mutual problem
- Say "and" rather than "but"
- State the integrative problem: How can we do both?

Brainstorming solutions and picking the best one
- Stay flexible
- Use tentative, exploratory language
- Agree on the best solution

Being firm when necessary: "firm flexibility"

Collaborating in groups
- Work with more, rather than less, information
- Develop multiple alternatives
- Create common goals
- Use humor
- Balance the power structure
- Seek consensus with qualification

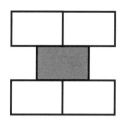

COMPROMISING

RECAPPING THE BASICS

Compromising occurs when you settle for a position that only partially satisfies your concerns and those of the other person. It is a win-lose mode in which you meet the other halfway—giving up something in order to gain some partial satisfaction.

Common examples
- "Soft" bargaining (exchanging concessions)
- Taking turns
- Moderating your conclusions

Benefits
- Pragmatism
- Speed and expediency
- Fairness
- Maintaining relationships

Costs
- Partially sacrificed concerns
- Suboptimal solutions
- Superficial understandings

Deciding When to Compromise

- Try not to compromise on vital issues
- Take turns bearing small costs
- Compromise on significant issues when competing and collaborating are not practical

Try Not to Compromise on Vital Issues

It is important to realize that compromise involves partial sacrifices for your (and the other person's) concerns. Some conflicts involve concerns so vital that even partial sacrifices would not be tolerable. Compromising on some conflict issues might bankrupt a company or undermine its ability to compete, for example, while others might undermine its integrity. On such important issues, try your utmost to use the two most assertive conflict-handling modes, competing and collaborating. Save compromise for concerns that are of *intermediate importance* to you—significant, but not vital.

Take Turns Bearing Small Costs

When you do someone a favor, the cost to you can be relatively small. (See "Deciding When to Accommodate," on pages 38–40.) However, when you do that person a series of favors, the cost may multiply to a point where you resent it. The total sacrifice becomes more significant to you and you may feel exploited. For that reason, it is important to make the sacrifices in a relationship as even as possible. Take turns bearing the cost, making sure you return each other's favors in a comparable way. Take turns picking up the check for business lunches, traveling to each other's work location, and so on.

Compromise on Significant Issues When Competing and Collaborating Are Not Practical

Compromising is the wise choice when it is impractical to try to fully satisfy your concerns and you can afford to settle for a "good enough" solution.

When people with equal power face a win-lose issue.

This is a common condition in conflicts over a fixed pie of resources—for example, in labor-management negotiations over prerogatives or pay. Collaborative solutions don't appear possible because the issue is inherently win-lose. With equal power, likewise, competing is unlikely to work—you don't have enough power to claim all the value. So you are left with compromise as the only practical approach.

When you need a temporary solution to a complex issue.

Sometimes the conflict issue is so complex that it will take much effort to find a good, permanent solution. Meanwhile, you can make a compromise decision so that work can continue: "For now, suppose we just . . ."

When you need an expedient decision under time pressure.

Here, there is no time to thoroughly work through a collaborative solution—or to have a lengthy debate. You may have other business that demands your attention or a rapidly approaching deadline. Notice, for example, that people are often more willing to compromise at the end of a meeting than at the beginning due to time constraints.

When more assertive modes would harm a relationship.

A quick compromise can take the stress off a relationship with a decision that is acceptable to both people. In a friendship, for example, it is considered rude to quibble over expenses, so a compromise is usually in order: "Let's split this one, shall we?" A quick compromise can also be useful on a significant issue when a relationship is at a vulnerable stage or when you're not sure you have the skills to work through a sensitive issue: "Suppose we just meet halfway on this?"

When competing and collaborating have failed.

Compromising is a good fallback strategy on significant issues when you have tried one of the more assertive modes and it hasn't worked. Because competing and collaborating are so fundamentally different, it is difficult to switch from one to the other. Compromise is usually the next best option when either fails: "We don't seem to be getting anywhere. Maybe we'd better think about a compromise."

Behavioral Skills for Compromising

- Moving from competing: making partial concessions
- Focusing on fairness: "principled" compromise

Moving from Competing: Making Partial Concessions

If you have been competing, compromise requires that both people let go of their initial positions and make sufficient partial concessions to get to an acceptable middle ground—without giving away the store.

Take stock of your situation.

When you've been competing and it hasn't been successful, it's tempting to try even stronger tactics (see the discussion of Competing). However, it is generally more useful to reassess your situation. The impasse you've reached indicates that your chances of winning are lower than you thought. What are the costs of continuing the impasse? What is likely to be the cost to your relationship? Would a compromise be acceptable to you and your organization? How much would you be willing to concede?

One factor in your willingness to make concessions is your *best alternative to a negotiated agreement,* or "BATNA" (Fisher & Ury, 1981). The better your alternative, the less willing you will probably be to compromise—and the smaller the concessions you will be willing to make. If you are selling something to the other person and know that you can get your asking price from someone else, you probably will not be willing to lower your price.

Suggest compromise without looking weak.

If you offer a compromise to a person who is still competing, it may encourage the other to hold out for greater concessions. If you decide that a compromise is in order, then, suggest it in a way that will not be mistaken for weakness. Use "we" language to point out the impasse and to suggest the value of compromise: "It looks like we're not getting anywhere. If we're going to meet this deadline, we'll probably have to start compromising. What do you think?"

Make partial concessions—as long as they are reciprocated.

Ask what the other is willing to settle for: "OK, what's your bottom line?" If that doesn't work, consider sharing a partial concession you would be willing to make *if it were reciprocated:* "I might be able to lower my asking price by $10,000 if you could raise your offer." Ask for a best counteroffer. If your new positions overlap, you have a compromise. If they don't, try

another round of partial concessions: "We're getting closer. Let's see if we can continue making progress."

Focusing on Fairness: "Principled" Compromise

Although the concession-making process is often necessary where competing has failed, it can strain relationships and lead to settlements based on bargaining skill rather than fairness. For that reason, many researchers recommend a more "principled" approach to compromise that is less adversarial.

Insist on a criterion of fairness up front.

The key is to agree on a criterion of fairness *before* you discuss all the facts of the issue: "Before we go any farther, let's decide what's fair. How about splitting any profits down the middle?" It is easier to agree in principle before you know precisely what the implications of the settlement will be. Agreeing on a criterion up front will also eliminate much of the conflict from the rest of the decision process. Examples of such agreement include basing a price on fair market value, relying on the judgment of someone you both respect, and dividing profits in proportion to the time each person has invested.

Determine the facts as objectively as possible.

Collect the information you need in order to apply your agreed-on criterion. Use neutral, objective sources. Have the property appraised by a neutral person. Ask your jointly chosen expert for his or her judgment. Calculate the profits and the time you both have invested in a project.

Apply the criterion.

At this point, the logic for the decision has been determined. All that remains may be a little arithmetic. If you do the math, make sure to have the other person check your work: "Per our agreement, the distribution of profits works out as follows . . ."

SUMMARY: WHEN AND HOW TO COMPROMISE

DECIDING WHEN TO COMPROMISE

Try not to compromise on vital issues

Take turns bearing small costs

Compromise on significant issues when competing and collaborating are not practical

- When people with equal power face a win-lose issue
- When you need a temporary solution to a complex issue
- When you need an expedient decision under time pressure
- When more assertive modes would harm a relationship
- When competing and collaborating have failed

BEHAVIORAL SKILLS FOR COMPROMISING

Moving from competing: making partial concessions

- Take stock of your situation
- Suggest compromise without looking weak
- Make partial concessions—as long as they are reciprocated

Focusing on fairness: "principled" compromise

- Insist on a criterion of fairness up front
- Determine the facts as objectively as possible
- Apply the criterion

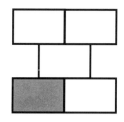

AVOIDING

RECAPPING THE BASICS

Avoiding occurs when you try not to engage in a conflict issue with the other person. It is a lose-lose mode in which you decide to pursue neither your own nor the other's concerns.

Common examples

- Avoiding people you find troublesome
- Not engaging issues that are unimportant, complex, or dangerous
- Postponing discussion until later

Benefits

- Reducing stress
- Saving time
- Steering clear of danger
- Setting up more favorable conditions

Costs

- Declining working relationships
- Resentment
- Delays
- Degraded communication and decision making

Deciding When to Avoid

- Try not to avoid people
- Avoid emotional conflicts
- Avoid issues where little can be gained
- Know when to postpone an issue

Try Not to Avoid People

It is usually easy to avoid people you dislike in purely social situations, where you are free to choose your own friends. However, in business and family situations, the consequences of avoiding people you dislike are more serious. In organizations, for example, being "professional" means putting up with some irritations in order to accomplish tasks. It also means putting effort into building and maintaining relationships rather than letting them deteriorate.

There are rare cases in which the costs of interacting with abusive or untrustworthy people are so high that avoiding is necessary for your own welfare and safety. This may mean seeking a transfer, finding another organization, or dissolving a marriage. But this is a last resort.

Avoid Emotional Conflicts

Research shows that effective groups deal with substantive conflict issues while avoiding so-called emotional conflicts. Emotional conflicts "personalize" the conflict and create defensiveness and hard feelings that can endure and put a severe strain on relationships. Here are some guidelines for avoiding emotional conflicts.

Avoid issues of blame.

When things don't turn out well, don't focus your energy on finding out who showed poor judgment, was negligent, or in general didn't do what he or she was supposed to do. Instead, figure out how the process can be improved to ensure a more successful outcome in the future.

Control your anger.

When people are angry, they tend to be righteous and to label the "offending" person's behavior in negative ways—for example, as irresponsible, lazy, or selfish. They may overgeneralize ("He always does that.") or try to hurt or punish the other person for his or her "transgression." Instead, find ways of controlling your anger. (See "Breaking the Anger Cycle," on pages 36–37.)

Don't discuss personalities.

Personalities are usually not changeable and evaluating them only makes people defensive, so don't waste your energy discussing them. Instead, negotiate over specific behaviors you would like to see changed. Rather than talk to someone about his rudeness with customers, for example, focus on the importance of making eye contact and saying "Thank you." Focusing on specific behaviors will force you to be more objective, as well as give the other person more useful information about what you want.

Avoid Issues Where Little Can Be Gained

Here are some common types of conflict issues that are not worth pursuing.

Issues that are unimportant.

Some issues are too trivial to attend to. In many cases, deciding what is unimportant will depend on what other issues are demanding your attention. For example, human relations issues are often avoided during a crisis situation.

Issues that are symptoms of other issues.

To get to the heart of an issue, you often have to first sort through the surface symptoms—for example, problems in a scheduling process are causing a number of subproblems, including gripes from people who did not get things when they needed them. Avoid spending a lot of time on symptoms that would take the discussion off on a tangent and away from the main issue—get past the gripes so you can fix the scheduling process.

Issues others can handle.

In general, avoid contributing when other people are able to resolve an issue well enough to allay your concerns. If you are a manager, likewise, try not to get involved in conflict issues your direct reports can handle on their own.

Issues that are too sensitive.

Salespeople have long been urged not to discuss politics or religion—both emotionally loaded issues. When deciding whether to address sensitive issues related to important business matters, weigh their importance against the risk to a relationship, as well as against your skill in dealing with such issues.

Issues you can't win.

Sometimes the cards are simply stacked against you. For example, if you know your boss would be adamantly opposed to a suggestion you are considering and that he has the power to veto it, you would be better off not pursuing it. You have little, if anything, to gain by bringing it up.

Know When to Postpone an Issue

In general, postpone addressing a significant issue when doing any of the following would improve your effectiveness.

Finding time.

You may be in the middle of dealing with other, more important, issues at the moment. If a new issue that arises is significant, postpone dealing with it until you have more time.

Gathering information.

Rather than make an immediate but uninformed decision in a conflict situation, postpone the discussion until you and the other person do your homework and have all the information you need. For example, you may need to check the regulations, make sure you have the authority, find out how Accounting has been handling such cases, track down a rumor, or run the numbers.

Refocusing.

Especially when you are dealing with complex or sensitive issues, it is vital that you be mentally alert and emotionally centered. Don't discuss conflict issues on Friday afternoon after a tough week, for example, or if one or the other person is upset or angry. Your chances of success will be greatly increased if you are at your best when you address the problem.

Taking a break.

When you and the other person feel stuck in your discussion and see no way out, it may be time to pause and sleep on it. Give your imagination the chance to come up with new alternatives.

Changing the setting.

Sometimes the physical setting is not conducive to a constructive discussion. You may be able to find a conference room that is quiet and feels neutral. For especially important and sensitive issues, you may prefer an off-site location that makes you feel even more at ease, such as a restaurant, a golf course, or even a fishing boat.

Behavioral Skills for Avoiding

- Deciding what is important
- Avoiding without being evasive
- Breaking the anger cycle

Deciding What Is Important

Avoiding unimportant issues is an inevitable part of focusing energy and attention. If you can decide what is important, you will have a logical basis for deciding which issues to avoid.

Be clear about your goals for a meeting.

If there is no clear goal, perhaps the meeting is a waste of time and you shouldn't be there.

Set joint goals if possible.

If you can agree on a shared rationale for a meeting, you will reduce the number of irrelevant issues that come up. With larger groups, use an agenda. With smaller groups, the process is less formal but still important: "Elizabeth, I'd like to try to resolve this overtime issue and make sure there are no hard feelings. Does that make sense as a goal for this meeting?"

Try to stick to those goals.

When a person strays from the main issues, remind him or her of the agenda: "Bob, I think we're getting away from our agenda." "Anne, you may want to talk with George about that later; right now can we get back to the pay issue?"

Be on the lookout for new information.

Watch for warning signs that avoided issues have become important enough to address:

- People have little energy for the issue on the agenda
- An avoided issue keeps coming up
- People are walking on eggshells over an issue that isn't being faced

Avoiding Without Being Evasive

Because it neglects the other person's concerns, avoiding can look like evading when the reason for it isn't clear. Avoiding can be seen as arbitrary and unfair and can lead to suspicions about your motives—for example, that you are punishing the other person, don't feel the other person is important, or have some hidden agenda. You can steer clear of these suspicions by using the following guidelines.

Give your reason.

Spell out the reason you are avoiding an issue: "Sorry, but I can't talk about this now. I have to be at a meeting across town in thirty minutes." "I think we should let Marketing handle this one. It seems to fall into their area of responsibility."

When postponing, set a time.

"Not now" is not a satisfactory response for most people. The clearest way to demonstrate that you are not evading an issue is to suggest a time to address it: "It's hard for me to even think about this now, with the upcoming inspection. Can this wait until the first of the month?" "It will take me some time to look this up. Let's get together again on Friday."

Use inviting language.

You can reduce the impression that your avoiding is arbitrary by involving the other person in the choice. Use language that invites the other person to avoid or postpone an issue: "I'm beginning to fade. Do you mind if we postpone this one until tomorrow?" "Why don't we check with Michelle and George and then get back together this afternoon?"

Breaking the Anger Cycle

The emotional conflicts described earlier follow a predictable pattern. Person A feels unfairly and deliberately injured or insulted by Person B. Person A becomes angry and expresses that anger in a way that Person B finds unfair and hurtful. Person B responds accordingly, and the anger and hurtful behavior escalate. Avoid emotional conflicts and break this destructive anger cycle by managing your behavior at key points.

Use your psychological boundaries.

Just as people have a physical skin that marks the boundary between their body and the physical environment, they also have a *psychological boundary.* Psychologists use this term to describe the dividing line between people and events in their social environment—their "psychological skin." We speak of people with weak psychological boundaries as being "thin-skinned." They are easily insulted or hurt and react automatically to those perceived insults. People with thicker skins do not react automatically to others'

behavior. They realize that they are responsible for their own emotions and find ways to control them.

- The Dalai Lama provided a useful metaphor. When someone insults you, it is as if they have thrown a spear that lands at your feet. You may pick it up and stab yourself with it, but why would you want to do that? The choice is yours.
- People with thicker skins tell themselves things like the following when they hear what sounds like an insult. "That's just Jerry being his typical, emotional self. It's not really about me. It's just him being him. But he is raising some important points that we can talk about."

Give the other person the benefit of the doubt.

You are more likely to become angry in a conflict situation when you see the other person as deliberately trying to hurt you or having an unflattering motive. People who are skilled at controlling their anger are reluctant to draw those kinds of conclusions. They try to give the other person the benefit of the doubt: "We're all doing the best we can here under the circumstances." They are careful not to "get inside the other person's head." ("You're trying to get even with me for what I said last week.") When the other person's motives are not clear, they ask rather than assume a motive: "Why do you say that?"

Discharge your anger safely.

If you do become angry, you will likely have an impulse to discharge your anger—to "get it off your chest." Once you discharge that anger, you will feel some relief and be able to think more clearly about the conflict issue. However, *it is dangerous to discharge your anger at the person you are angry with.* Discharge your anger by discussing it with a third party—a co-worker whom you trust, a friend, or a family member. Discuss the issue with the other person only *after* you have regained perspective.

Watch your connotations.

Most words that describe people have good/bad overtones. Using words with negative connotations is one of the main ways people try to hurt each other when they are angry. For that reason, steer clear of words with negative connotations when discussing the other person—or his or her behavior—in a conflict and use more neutral and specific language. For example, rather than labeling the other's behavior as "lazy," talk about specifics: "I'm concerned that you haven't taken much initiative on this project." Instead of talking about another department's "negligence," talk about the specific action that they didn't take that needs to be taken in the future.

Use humor to defuse tension.

Humor can help defuse tension and deescalate a threatening situation. It can introduce a sense of playfulness and comradeship. It also provides a way of saying things in an indirect manner without raising people's defenses. Here's an example.

> Jim gets worked up in a meeting and makes an angry, "showstopping" comment that ends with: "Dammit, *this stuff is killing us!*" Rather than attack his statement head-on, other group members say things like: "So, Jim, I can't tell—do you feel strongly about this?" "Yeah, Jim, don't pussyfoot around here." "I'd rate that last comment about an 8 on the Richter scale. Maybe 8.6." Jim, slightly embarrassed, tones down his rhetoric and says, "OK, maybe I got a little carried away. But it does seem important to look at this issue." Crisis averted, the discussion resumes.

SUMMARY: WHEN AND HOW TO AVOID

DECIDING WHEN TO AVOID

Try not to avoid people

Avoid emotional conflicts
- Avoid issues of blame
- Control your anger
- Don't discuss personalities

Avoid issues where little can be gained
- Issues that are unimportant
- Issues that are symptoms of other issues
- Issues others can handle
- Issues that are too sensitive
- Issues you can't win

Know when to postpone an issue
- Finding time
- Gathering information
- Refocusing
- Taking a break
- Changing the setting

BEHAVIORAL SKILLS FOR AVOIDING

Deciding what is important
- Be clear about your goals for a meeting
- Set joint goals if possible
- Try to stick to those goals
- Be on the lookout for new information

Avoiding without being evasive
- Give your reason
- When postponing, set a time
- Use inviting language

Breaking the anger cycle
- Use your psychological boundaries
- Give the other person the benefit of the doubt
- Discharge your anger safely
- Watch your connotations
- Use humor to defuse tension

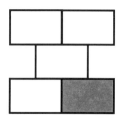

ACCOMMODATING

RECAPPING THE BASICS

Accommodating occurs when you seek or accept a position that would meet the other person's concerns at the expense of your own. It is a win-lose mode in which you neglect or sacrifice your own concerns in favor of the other's.

Common examples
- Doing a favor to help someone
- Being persuaded
- Obeying an authority
- Deferring to another's expertise
- Appeasing someone who is dangerous

Benefits
- Helping someone out
- Restoring harmony
- Building relationships
- Choosing a quick ending

Costs
- Sacrificed concerns
- Loss of respect
- Loss of motivation

Deciding When to Accommodate

- Don't fall into a pattern of appeasement
- Yield to a better position
- Concede when you are overruled or losing
- Make a small sacrifice when it's important to others
- Accommodate to clean up hard feelings

Don't Fall into a Pattern of Appeasement

There are times when it may be dangerous for you not to appease someone. For example, your professional welfare may be threatened by a boss who is emotionally out of control and verbally abusive. Perhaps he has been having a bad day and is at the end of his rope. "That's it!" he shouts. "I've had it with you people. Just do it or don't bother coming in on Monday!" Although you don't deserve this treatment, you appease him while he's out of control.

However, do not allow this sort of threat and appeasement to become a pattern—in any relationship. It won't be healthy for you, and your appeasement will likely encourage further instances of rage and threats. Try to bring up the episode at a later date, when the other person is not out of control, and explain its costs for you. If it happens again, look for another position. If the first episode was severe, don't wait for a second episode.

Yield to a Better Position

Sometimes you make the case for your position, hear others' positions, and conclude that you are probably wrong. When that happens, the only honest option is to admit it. In the long run, this admission does more to build your credibility than does defending a shaky position. It is also in the best interests of your organization.

When you are persuaded.

In some cases, you encounter information that convinces you that you are wrong. You see that you missed some important point or consideration. You reevaluate and find that you now agree with the other person's position, so you admit it.

When others know more and there's little time.

In crisis or emergency situations, you may find your position opposed by people with more experience on the issue. When there isn't time for others to convince you of their position, you may have to defer to people with greater knowledge or expertise, in the belief that their position is probably best.

Concede When You Are Overruled or Losing

Sometimes you make your best case for your position, hear opposing arguments, and still believe in the merits of your own position—but you find that your position isn't going to prevail. When you realize this, it's time to concede gracefully. Otherwise, you risk delaying the decision unnecessarily and losing goodwill.

When you are overruled by your boss.

If push comes to shove and you are overruled on an issue, it is usually in your best interest (and the organization's) to respect the hierarchy and comply. To do otherwise is to risk being seen as insubordinate by your boss and those at higher organizational levels. "Going over your boss's head" is very risky in most organizations

unless there are clear violations of law or organizational policy involved.

When you are outvoted in a group.

Larger groups usually find it necessary to make decisions using simple majority rule. Smaller groups are more effective when they make decisions by consensus. Under rules of consensus, you as a member have the right to keep talking until you are convinced that the other people understand your position and your reasoning. If that happens but the group still fails to support your position, you are obliged to submit to the group's position.

When you are outmatched and losing.

Often it doesn't make sense to wait until the final decision is made before you concede. When it becomes clear that your position won't prevail, you may want to stop pushing your position in order to save time and put less strain on relationships.

Make a Small Sacrifice When It's Important to Others

There are many times when, with a small sacrifice to yourself, you can do a greater good for someone else. Make such sacrifices when you can afford them—that is, when the cost is relatively low—and when you care about the other person or want to build a relationship with him or her.

Doing favors.

Favors are helpful acts you perform for others that go beyond what is required or ordinary. For example, another department head might ask to borrow some of your people to help with a crisis. Or a good customer might ask for an extension on a bill because her company's accounting systems are down.

Letting people test their wings.

When you delegate decisions to people who report to you, they often make different decisions than you would. To help those people develop, you may need to let them carry out those decisions even though you have doubts. This form of accommodation makes sense only when the potential costs of a bad decision are not very high or when there is plenty of time to recover from it. Support these decisions and keep abreast of how they are working out.

Boosting confidence.

When your own status and self-confidence are relatively secure, you can afford to be self-effacing to boost the confidence of others. For example, you might tell one of your direct reports that you could not have handled a project as well as he did. In introducing that same project at a meeting of your peers, you might give him most of the credit, even though it was your idea in the first place.

Accommodate to Clean Up Hard Feelings

Some important acts of accommodating occur in the aftermath of previous conflicts—to repair strained relationships and allow you to move forward.

To repair damage you have caused.

The other person may have hard feelings toward you because of something you did—damage you did, competing behavior, or angry comments. Left unresolved, these resentments can damage your relationship with this person, undermining goodwill and trust. If the relationship is important to you, you may need to apologize and make reparations. (See "Satisfying a Complaint," on page 41.)

To forgive others so you can move on.

If you feel you were wronged by someone else in a past conflict, you may be holding a grudge—feeling resentment, bitterness, and probably hostility. You may have fantasies about getting even or perhaps forcing the other person to apologize, but you realize that this is unlikely to happen. In this situation, it usually pays to forgive the other person—to let go of your grudge so that you can move on. This doesn't mean you fully trust the other person. You can still be wary of a repeat offense. But let go of the bitterness that ties up your energy and damages the quality of your life.

Behavioral Skills for Accommodating

- Conceding gracefully
- Planting seeds
- Satisfying a complaint

Conceding Gracefully

There is more at stake than your position. When you find it necessary to concede, do it in a way that preserves credibility and goodwill.

Don't be a sore loser.

You may be frustrated about having to concede, but try not to get angry about it. The hallmarks of a sore loser are all too familiar: stomping away in a fit of temper and making dire predictions ("You'll be sorry!"), demeaning comments ("*Somebody* had to be big enough to give in here"), or complaints of unfairness ("We were cheated!"). Take a higher road that will earn you respect.

Explain your motives.

Your accommodating could be misinterpreted as a sign that you don't care about the issue, are yielding to pressure, or weren't sure of your position. Therefore it is helpful to *briefly* state your reasons for doing so. "I find Harry's new data convincing." "Much as I would like us to do this, I can see that I don't have the votes." "In the interest of time, I'll withdraw my motion."

Planting Seeds

Some of your concerns may require long campaigns to be successfully met. For example, instituting important changes often requires others to learn new ways of thinking, implement a new vocabulary, and let go of old habits. You can usually expect resistance and initial setbacks when you propose such changes, but keep your eye on the longer-term campaign. Even though you may have to concede on some early decisions, you can still lay the groundwork for future success. Use the early episodes to plant new ideas, new information, and a new vocabulary, which will gradually change the way others look at an issue.

For example, suppose your engineering group prides itself on its problem-solving precision. However, you are concerned that it spends too much time finding precise solutions to problems where a "good enough" solution would do. You start pointing out the difference between "precision" issues and "good enough" issues. At first the group keeps using its old approach, but before long it begins to use your terms and implements a quicker decision process on the "good enough" issues.

Satisfying a Complaint

Complaints provide feedback that can help improve performance. Handling them effectively can also repair damaged relationships with friends and co-workers—and restore customer loyalty. Still, handling complaints is often challenging and sensitive.

Accept anger (but not abuse).

Complaints are often accompanied by anger. View the anger as part of the other's frustration, not as a personal attack. (See "Use your psychological boundaries," on page 36.) Convey the attitude that it is all right for the other person to be angry. While abuse—including screaming, name-calling, physical threats, and hostile physical contact—is not acceptable, expressing heated words is okay. For example, saying, "Your people knocked down our fence! How could they do that? Don't you train them?" is simply an expression of anger.

When you accept other people's anger, you let them "get it off their chest." As they express that anger (without your being defensive or counterattacking), they gradually discharge it. You will notice a change in their tone and posture: you will hear less intensity, and they will begin to relax. Until that happens, it will be difficult for them to hear what you say. After it happens, you can discuss things more reasonably. Often, people will even be apologetic about their angry behavior of a few minutes ago.

Explain (but don't defend) what happened.

The people who are complaining often don't understand how the offending action could have occurred. Assuming the action was deliberate, careless, or even stupid will intensify their anger and damage your reputation with them. Provide information about any mitigating circumstances that can help explain what happened: "We have been having problems with our computers." "The person who normally handles your account has been on sick leave." "The driver was trying to avoid hitting a dog." Be careful not to defend what happened or try to talk the other person out of his or her complaint. If the person suffered a loss, he or she has a right to complain.

Use active listening.

There are times when it is not clear what the other person wants—especially when the person is a child or someone who is upset. When it's not clear what the person wants, use active listening skills to make sure you understand the position he or she is taking. "So you would like us to repair your fence. Is that right?"

Apologize.

People who complain usually want an apology and assurance that whatever happened won't happen again. A timely apology can go a long way toward smoothing a conflict situation. When you apologize, you are acknowledging the damage done, taking responsibility for your part in it, and expressing regret. The implicit message is that you are not the kind of person (or organization) that does that kind of thing, you regret that it happened, and you won't let it happen again. You are hoping for forgiveness and a restoration of trust.

Make reparations when appropriate.

When the other person's interests have suffered, you may need to go beyond an apology. You may offer a gift as a symbolic repayment or provide more complete compensation. For example, hotel personnel may adjust a bill to make up for a malfunctioning shower. And you should offer to repair the fence your driver knocked down.

SUMMARY: WHEN AND HOW TO ACCOMMODATE

DECIDING WHEN TO ACCOMMODATE	*BEHAVIORAL SKILLS FOR ACCOMMODATING*

Don't fall into a pattern of appeasement

Yield to a better position
- When you are persuaded
- When others know more and there's little time

Concede when you are overruled or losing
- When you are overruled by your boss
- When you are outvoted in a group
- When you are outmatched and losing

Make a small sacrifice when it's important to others
- Doing favors
- Letting people test their wings
- Boosting confidence

Accommodate to clean up hard feelings
- To repair damage you have caused
- To forgive others so you can move on

Conceding gracefully
- Don't be a sore loser
- Explain your motives

Planting seeds

Satisfying a complaint
- Accept anger (but not abuse)
- Explain (but don't defend) what happened
- Use active listening
- Apologize
- Make reparations when appropriate

REFERENCES

Blake, Robert R., & Mouton, Jane S. (1964). *The managerial grid*. Houston: Gulf.

Eisenhardt, Kathleen, Kahwajy, Jean L., & Burgeois, L. J., III. (1997). How top management team can have a good fight. *Harvard Business Review, 75*(4), 77–85.

Fisher, Roger, & Ury, William. (1981). *Getting to YES: Negotiating agreement without giving in*. Boston: Houghton Mifflin.

Johnson, David W., & Johnson, Frank P. (2000). *Joining together: Group theory and group skills* (7th ed.). Boston: Allyn & Bacon.

Lax, David A., & Sebenius, James K. (1986). *The manager as negotiator.* New York: Free Press.

Pruitt, Dean G., & Rubin, Jeffrey Z. (1986). *Social conflict: Escalation, stalemate, and settlement.* New York: Random House.

Another TKI Resource

Thomas, Kenneth W., & Thomas, Gail F. (2004). *Introduction to Conflict and Teams*. Sunnyvale, CA: The Myers-Briggs® Company.

This booklet focuses on the conflict-handling modes in a team setting. It helps people understand their team member conflict style and provides detailed guidance on how to improve their effectiveness in dealing with teammates. It also helps identify your team's conflict style and suggests ways that teams with different styles can improve their effectiveness.

ABOUT THE AUTHOR

KEN THOMAS is known internationally for his contributions to the literature on conflict management. He has written a number of classic articles on the five conflict-handling modes. He is coauthor, with Ralph Kilmann, of the *Thomas-Kilmann Conflict Mode Instrument* (TKI), which has sold millions of copies and has been translated into several languages. His award-winning video for CRM Films, *Dealing with Conflict*, is also a top seller.

Thomas's work combines respected academic research with practical training and consulting. Besides the TKI, he has coauthored training instruments including the *Power Base Inventory,* the *Stress Resiliency Profile,* and the *Work Engagement Profile*—all published by The Myers-Briggs® Company. Thomas is also the author of *Intrinsic Motivation at Work* (Berrett-Koehler, 2000). He is a frequent speaker at professional conferences.